Wildlife A-Z

A Treasure Trove of Creature Fun Facts

Text and Illustration By Nathan Earley

ISBN:

978-1727246889

To my loving parents, Luella and Bill, and sister, Amanda for their unwavering support of my artistic endeavors.

A is for antelope, long and slender…

B is for beaver, a constant lodge mender.

C is for camel, complete with a hump…

D is for dolphin, seen swimming in a pod or clump.

E is for elephant, large with grace…

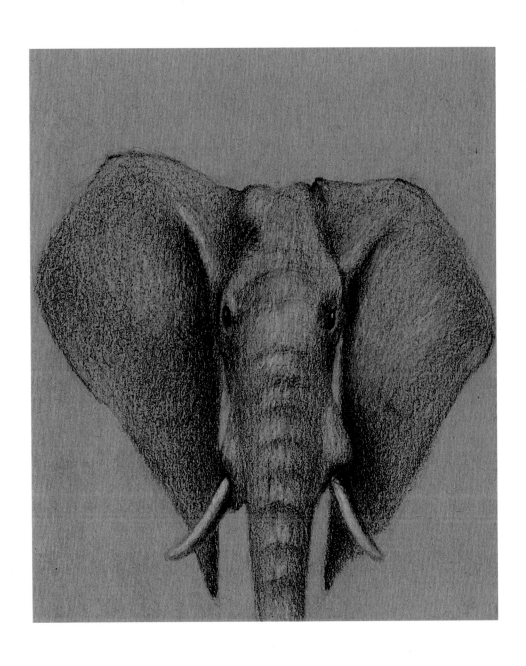

F is for frog, eyes bulging from its face.

G is for giraffe, with a long, long
neck…

H is for hare, in the distance, a speck.

I is for iguana, exotic and rare…

J is for jaguar, spots on fur here and there.

K is for kangaroo, leaping so high…

L is for lion, eyeing its prey pass by.

M is for mouse, small and meek…

N is for newt, a land and water dwelling sneak.

O is for otter, with a weasel-like feature...

P is for panther, a dark and haunting creature.

Q is for quail, gathering twigs for a nest…

R is for raccoon, scrounging for food, a constant pest.

S is for seal, smooth and sleek…

T is for tiger, anything but weak.

U is for upupa, a European bird…

V is for vulture, soaring with a second or third.

W is for walrus, long tusks and all…

X is for xerus, a squirrel, slight and small.

Y is for yak, an ox of the middle east…

Z is for zebra, a black and white beast.

Made in the USA
Columbia, SC
16 October 2018